OZARK COUNTY HEART
Boyhood Memories of a Dora Missouri Farm

2020 DORA BOYS BASKETBALL CHAMPIONSHIP UPDATE EDITION

© 2017 Martin Capages, Jr.

All rights reserved. No part of this book may be reproduced or utilized in any form or by any means, electronic or mechanical, including photocopying, recording or by any information storage retrieval system without permission in writing from the publisher, except for a reviewer who may quote brief passages in a review to be printed in a newspaper, magazine or electronic publication.

American Freedom Publications LLC

www.americanfreedompublications.com

2638 E. Wildwood Road

Springfield, Missouri 65804

ISBN 978-1-64136-608-3   Paperback Version

Cover Design   Christopher M. Capages

www.capagescreative.com

Final Manuscript Editor   Pamela Kay Capages

First Edition October 15, 2017 Updated April 15, 2020

Printed in the United States of America

DEDICATION

This book is dedicated to my 7th and 8th grade teacher, Mr. James Windell Hall, and to the People of Ozark County Missouri.

ACKNOWLEDGEMENTS

I am grateful for the support of Norene Prososki and Sue Ann Jones of the Ozark County Times in the initial publication of these boyhood recollections. I also want to thank Mary Collins and the Dora School Library for helping with the many yearbook photographs used in this book. And finally, I want to thank my wife, Pamela Kay Capages, for her encouragement during the process and for making the final edit of the manuscript.

For this updated version, I want to thank KY3 Ozarks Sports Zone for permission to republish Kai Raymer's article *Falcons make Dora basketball history, win first-ever Class 1 state championship*. Go Falcons.

OZARK COUNTY HEART
Boyhood Memories of a Dora Missouri Farm

FOREWORD

In each year's "Real Ozarks Magazine" we describe Ozark County as a special place with a remarkable heritage. It *is* a special place – but it's not always easy to live here. It takes a hearty constitution and a lot of gumption to survive in a place where the summers are hot, the winters can be icy, the roads are crooked, the economy struggles and the facilities are few. We've got ticks, chiggers, snakes, mosquitoes, poison ivy and Lord knows what other challenges. But what many folks find is that, once they've lived here, it's hard to live anywhere else. Many former Ozark Countians – Martin Capages among them – find that Ozark County memories stay in their hearts forever.

Like many modern-day Ozark Countians, Martin's family was an unlikely match for hillbilly life, yet they not only survived but still look fondly upon the memories of the hard life on their hardscrabble Ozarks farm.

Martin's dad, a Marine Corps retiree, grew up in New York City, for heaven's sake, about as far from hillbilly living as anyone could get! And his mother, a farm girl from Tennessee, had experienced enough of the rigors of the family-farm lifestyle to know it wasn't her dream come true in adulthood. Yet there they were in 1956, settling on 80 acres of rocks and weeds in the northeastern corner of Ozark County, which had then (and still has today) fewer than 10,000 residents, total.

Martin colorfully describes the shock of the family of six moving into a two-bedroom farmhouse that was heated by a wood-burning stove and had one of the few inside bathrooms in the Dora community. (He especially came to value that "luxury" when he arrived at Dora School to find outhouses for toilets.)

Still, Martin recalls the details of his childhood adventures with affection and a sense of accomplishment. Some of the scenes he describes are a little difficult to read. (I admit to grimacing as I read his description of his dad neutering the family's two cats. But I appreciate that he was writing about a procedure that's common on most farms, at least when it's performed on cattle, if not on cats.)

I loved the way he expressed admiration for the small-school teachers who inspired him, and I laughed reading about his misadventures on the Cub tractor and his "nemesis, the barnyard pond." Then I grieved with him as he recalled the family's retreat from Ozark County to Tennessee, where his dad sold encyclopedias door to door, and where Martin held his beloved dog Tripoli as the cherished pet fell ill due to poison.

But then they were back in Ozark County for a second go-round of hillbilly living, and Martin picks up the family's Ozark County saga as though the interruption had never happened, writing about doing the chores many of us Ozark County kids grew up doing, as well as the pranks he and his friends pulled off without being caught – or didn't. So many of us can identify with his having to wear clothes he hated (and modified himself at school), flying over the hilly, two-lane roads with a 14-year-old driver at the wheel, and learning life lessons not only on the farm but also at the traveling carnival, on the basketball court or at the roller-skating rink.

In "Ozark County Heart," Martin shares vivid recollections of his family's brief but unforgettable time on their little farm near Dora, and in doing so he captures the challenging, confounding and wonderful essence of Ozark County. It is a place like no other, and it has a way of settling into the hearts of those who've lived here. Then, no matter how many years and miles intervene, hillbilly memories keep pulling those hearts back home.

Sue Ann Jones
Ozark County Times

TABLE OF CONTENTS

DEDICATION iii
ACKNOWLEDGEMENTS iv
FOREWORD v
Preface ix
Chapter 1. The Capages Clan 1
Chapter 2. Getting Started 3
Chapter 3 Mechanical Advantage 6
Chapter 4 School is in Session 7
Chapter 5. Reading, Writing, 'Rithmetic and Softball 9
Chapter 6. First Fall 13
Chapter 7. Hunting and Fishing Country Style 15
Chapter 8. The First Winter 16
Chapter 9. Spring At Last 19
Chapter 10. Missouri Summers are Hot 21
Chapter 11. Tennessee Detour 23
Chapter 12 Back to Dora 24
Chapter 13. Return to Windell Hall's eighth grade class 26
Chapter 14. I Get Wheels. 28
Chapter 15. A Dora Freshman 30
Chapter 16. Learning How Not To Gamble 33
Chapter 17. Basketball 34
Chapter 18. Gypsies Again 36
YEAR BOOK PHOTOS 37
FIFTY YEARS LATER 43
REUNION 45
DORA WINS 2020 STATE CHAMPIONSHIP 51
IN MEMORIUM 54

OZARK COUNTY HEART
Boyhood Memories of a Dora Missouri Farm

PREFACE

My siblings and I were not farm kids. We were Marine Corps brats and thought that milk came out of a carton. But Dad left the Marines in 1956 and dragged us to the Ozarks in Missouri. To listen to my three younger sisters and me reminisce about our life on the Dora Farm, you would have thought we were there all our lives, but it was just a couple of years from late summer 1956 to January 1959.

Now Mom was a farm girl from Millington, Tennessee, the youngest daughter of a family with 13 kids. Going back to farm life was not on her bucket list. And Dad, well he grew up in New York City, the son of Greek emigrants. He knew nothing about farming but he could always read about how to farm, so that was all he needed.

During one of our many family relocations from East to West Coasts during Dad's career as a Marine Captain, in 1954 we stayed in a little town on the Taneycomo River called Branson, Missouri. Mom and Dad must have fallen in love with the place. Two years later, there we were with Strout Realty in Branson scouring the area for a farm. They found one near a little town called Dora, Missouri, population 100. A long, long winding way from Branson.

The farm was on eighty acres of rolling, rocky hills with three ponds, two pastures, an apple orchard and a stand of black walnut trees. It was beautiful. The farm house was small with two bedrooms and one of the only inside bathrooms in Dora with a flushing toilet and running hot and cold water. There was a milking barn and some old out-buildings built of oak plank and local stone. Behind the house was a remarkable ice storage house with one-foot thick, hollow walls filled with sawdust as insulation.

There was no central heating. Heat came from a wooden stove in the middle of the living room. More about that later.

There is so much I want to describe about this formative time in our lives, mine, in particular, that I am overcome with waves of nostalgia. But God put this time in my life for His own purpose. As I grow older, His reasons become more mysterious. But, I will love the people of Dora and Ozark County forever.

Martin Capages, Jr. PhD

OZARK COUNTY HEART
Boyhood Memories of a Dora Missouri Farm

CHAPTER 1. THE CAPAGES CLAN

There were six of us. Mom (Helen), Dad (Martin Sr.) the oldest boy (me) and my three sisters, Candy, Chery and Krissy. We arrived at the farm in Dora when I was just turning 12. Candy was nearly 9, Chery 8 and Krissy was 2-1/2.

My first observations were the bugs. In Southern California there were no wasps or grasshoppers as far as I knew. Now here in Missouri the sky was full of red and black wasps, there were waves of grasshoppers and stink bugs crawled on the window screens. As we rolled down the gravel roads in our new, green Plymouth station wagon, the dust poured in through the open rear window. Candy was in the back, crying about something while her tears made rivulets in the dust on her cheeks. Chery was curled up asleep next to her, nearly invisible in a thin coating of gravel dust. Welcome to the Missouri countryside.

My mother was no slacker. She knew farm work was hard and never ending. But she was a Marine officer's wife and lovingly obedient. So she called on her skills from Tennessee while Dad read books from the Missouri Conservation Service. They were the new Noah and dutiful wife. Time to fill the Ark.

This photo of the Capages family was taken on a late summer day in 1956 when they left California to move to Dora. From left, the dad, Martin Capages Sr.; Chery, 8; Candy, nearly 9; Krissy, 2 1/2; Martin Jr. almost 12; and the kids' mother, Helen Capages

CHAPTER 2. GETTING STARTED

My memory is a bit hazy on this, but I believe our first purchase was a cow, a gorgeous light brown and white Guernsey Dad named Bossie. Bossie was as gentle as could be. Her horns had been tipped by her previous owner and she became our pet. She would follow me through the apple orchard, eating apples from my hand or off the ground. Dad learned how to milk a cow with poor Bossie as the guinea pig. She became a little less friendly after Dad installed a milking machine and Bossie was the first customer.

Next came the chickens, lots and lots of chickens. Corn went in one end, and chicken poop came out the other. Candy learned how to feed the chicks, Chery would follow right behind trying to copy her sister but less organized. A sign of things to come. Krissy would learn to play with the pullets just like her baby dolls, even pushing them around in her baby stroller. That was the beginning of the domestic animal life.

Next came the pigs, one boar and two sow. Dad did all the work as far as the livestock were concerned, I hadn't even started into puberty and was not strong enough or mature enough yet to be useful in his eyes. He was right. My sisters and I were still playing with toys together. We merged my Army men with Candy's Fort Apache figures. It was a grand time. Rin Tin Tin was big on the TV and we re-enacted many episodes. There were some of own stories built around the little plastic figures. One character was a cowboy that was supposed to be sitting on a chuck wagon. We didn't have the chuck wagon so he always looked bent over. We named him "Ben Dover".

That first summer was a delight. We climbed the apple trees and ate apples right off the tree. There were Winesaps, Red and Yellow Delicious, and Grannie Greens. We even had peach trees, but the peaches were often wormy.

A local farmer loaned us an old dark brown mare called Mert or Myrt. Mert bucked me and Candy off when Candy touched her withers by mistake. Actually, Mert was very gentle. Candy was sitting behind me. I had leaned forward and Candy leaned forward bringing her heels along Mert's withers. I will never forget seeing those hooves going past our heads as she threw us off. We never told Dad but Candy was hooked on horses from then on. Krissy got a little too close to Mert once and got her foot caught under Mert's hoof. Krissy said "Off horse, off". That was that.

The love of my life then was our beautiful Black and Tan Doberman, Tripoli. She was perfect. Both smart, gentle and protective. She was also a city kid, just like us. The country was amazing to her and Dad let her roam. But we had another dog too. He was a little, mongrel wire-hired terrier named Peanuts. He was

Candy's dog. She should've named him Alfie. He quickly met all the ladies for miles around. And he got in trouble with Dad when he killed a chicken. Dad cured that trait quickly. He tied the dead chicken to Peanut's collar and made him drag it around until it rotted off. It worked, but it took weeks before Peanut's aroma was acceptable. But, his lady friends still loved him.

Two cats joined us next. The first was a black and white beauty with a black spot above his lip similar to Marilyn Monroe's. Chery named him Inky. Then Dad brought home a thoroughbred Siamese. We named him Thai. These two feline brothers were meant to be members of the Capages Clan. But they would pay a price.

The next arrival was a Jersey cow we named Susie. She was more aloof than Bossie. I remember that Jerseys gave white milk and Guernsey milk was more yellowish with more butterfat. Bossie would often eat wild onions and bitter weed. It tainted her milk something awful.

The next arrivals were the Angus. These are beef cattle and not friendly. I don't remember how many we had but the leader was a cow we named China Doll. She would only answer to my Dad.

That completed the passenger list on the Capages Ark for the first leg of the journey.

CHAPTER 3 MECHANICAL ADVANTAGE

Every boy remembers driving a car for the first time. For farm boys, it is a tractor. Ours was a brand new Farmall Cub with "Cultivision". Cultivision meant the seat was offset to the right so you could see the furrows. We had a single disc plow on the  right side just in front of the driver. It made a beautiful deep single furrow. It didn't take long for Dad to decide I could handle the Cub. At first he used the Tom Sawyer "whitewash fence" approach. Sure, it was fun to drive around freely, but plowing single furrows side by side is another matter. It is boring and hot. In late summer the sweat bees would get in the creases of your skin and sting with each movement. But the Cub was safe to drive since it had a wide stance. A 13 year old boy could handle it.

My first chore was plowing the northeast 20 acres in order to plant oats. There is no power steering and the 13-year old city kid started to build some biceps and grow calluses on his hands.

CHAPTER 4 SCHOOL IS IN SESSION

H. G. Wells must have set the Time Machine back 50 years, especially between California time and Dora time. Mom and Dad rounded up the kids and took us to Dora elementary school. We were used to the modern, progressive California schools with its home room, hall lockers and athletic facilities.

Now I joined the combined 7th and 8th Grade class of Mr. Windell Hall. The class room had the 7th graders on one side, the 8th graders on the other, separated by the wood fired pot belly stove just in front of Mr. Hall's desk. It was still warm outside so the stove was empty. It would become very important later on. My Dad and Windell (he always went by Windell) hit it off from the start. Windell Hall was a remarkable teacher. He had a Master's degree from Southwest Missouri State (now Missouri State University). I owe my academic successes, especially in mathematics and English to Windell. More about that later.

Now the big shock. There were no indoor bathrooms. The "facilities" were a row of outhouses on the north edge of the school grounds. One of my classmates, Stan Adams, lost one of his shoes in those facilities. He wasn't going in after it and just walked around with one shoe on the rest of the day. The playground was the open field on the south end of the school grounds. There was a softball field and two poles with basketball goals with dirt courts, no nets. There was no gymnasium.

At lunch time, we usually had peanut butter and jelly sandwiches wrapped in waxed paper and maybe a banana that Mom packed in a brown paper bag. Every now and then I got to buy my lunch at the Osborne's store just adjacent to the school grounds on the west side. You could get a hamburger for ten cents. It was just a hamburger patty between two pieces of white sandwich bread, a pickle and mustard. Stan Adams watched the cook feed a dog behind the counter near the grill then go back to cooking, no hand washing of course. Just added to the flavor I guess.

The 7th and 8th grades did have one class outside the home room, Mr. William Wood's music class. I will never forget that first meeting with Mr. Wood, he said "hmm, CAPAGES, is that Greek?" I knew I was in the presence of another intelligent man in this 50-year-old time capsule. Mr. Wood and Pat Hambelton would be my sisters' main teachers. They would be in great hands.

CHAPTER 5. READING, WRITING, 'RITHMETIC AND SOFTBALL

Windell Hall loved baseball. But the 7th and 8th grades were restricted to softball. A lot of my most memorable times revolved around this sport. The first involved the morning recesses in early September. I would play catch with Billy Leroy, Tommy Shipley and Clifton Shipley. I didn't have a decent ball glove. It was a kid's glove with open fingers. Everyone knew a good ball glove had web fingers, I was always embarrassed but then we got some new gloves through the school athletic fund. We shared these and I marked mine with my name. It was first come first served, but I managed to get mine most of the time.

We would spend recess playing catch or catching flies hit by the 8th graders and high school boys. For refreshment, we got in line at the cooler for chocolate milk. The milk came in little glass bottles with tin foil lids. You would punch your thumb through the foil and glug. It was almost always good except one time. Louise McDonald got a bottle where the milk had curdled. I was fond of Louise and her BFFs, Juanita Cudworth and Lula Collins. They were always kind to me. Louise would usually get in line behind me and touch my elbow so I wouldn't back up over her (I think). That day she should have been in front of me, I got the last bottle of good chocolate milk.

As I said, recesses were just the warm ups for our 45 minute physical education class. PE was slow pitch softball with Windell Hall always pitching for both sides. This eventually became the 7th grade ball team. We even traveled to other schools to play. Windell then had to have a student pitch and Billy Leroy got the job. I liked to play second base but Windell kept putting me at third base because I was the only one brave enough (or dumb enough) to catch the throw from our catcher, Clifford Hensley. Clifford was much older than the rest of us and his cut off throw to third base broke the speed of sound. We put a lot of third base runners out. And I had to ice my thumb and fingers between innings.

Being able to catch Clifford's throw had some positive effects when we graduated to the eighth grade. The Dora colors were red and white. I needed a ball cap and could only find a blue one at Paul Roy's dry goods store. We didn't have uniforms anyway so I played wearing my blue cap on the 8th grade team. I knew I had become a bit of a hero when a few weeks later all the 7th grade team players were wearing blue ball caps. Well, maybe I thought I was a hero. Could have been that Roy's store only carried blue caps. I like my version better.

Baseball was king in Dora. The 1956 World Series was no exception. The teachers and students all gathered around one TV in principal Mearl Bell's office and on October 8, 1956 we watched Don Larsen pitch the only World Series no hitter in history. The Yankees beat the Brooklyn Dodgers in Game 5. I will never forget watching Yogi Berra run out to the mound and jump on Larsen to celebrate. That day we played softball until dark. No classes.

But there was plenty of disciplined learning in the 7th grade. We had math, science, English, American History and that awful Missouri history and government class. We read in the Weekly Reader about this revolutionary leader named Castro in Cuba. He was trying to overthrow the dictator, Batista. Dad said he met Batista or his son at some Marine event in Florida. Something about an artillery demonstration. I didn't know Dad had ever been in Florida.

We also read about the growth of a religion called Islam. But there was no World History class or even a class on geography. But I still remember the photo of a woman wearing a hijab in the Weekly Reader.

William Wood's music classes were a hoot, especially if I could sit next to Eula May Parsons. That meant beating Ronnie Thornton to the seat next to the Preacher's daughter.

Since the 7th and 8th grade classes were in the same room, we 7th grade boys could ogle the more mature 8th grade girls. Top of my list were Aleta Smith and Scharlotte Martin. But the 8th grade boys kept us in check. Especially Kelly Martin and Lonnie Johnson. Both guys had Ricky Nelson good looks including the hair. But Kelly Martin was "The Man" and my hero. He was dating Velvie Jean Bird, a gorgeous high school freshman. Kelly and Candy's dog, Peanuts, were kindred spirits as far as the Ladies were concerned.

Now I think Kelly Martin and Scharlotte Martin were cousins or so I was told. Scharlotte was a fashion star. I remember her wearing the first sack dress, it was brown or perhaps light green. Maybe she had two. It made quite a stir. Her older sister, Virginia 'Gene' was a beauty, especially on skates. Enough about the girls for now.

CHAPTER 6. FIRST FALL

In school, softball season was over. Now we played basketball on the dirt courts. The earlier the better. The frozen earth was okay, but by noon it was a mess. Some mornings were warm, then the next morning was frigid. There was a drizzle one day at recess and we had recess anyway. As we went out into the now dead grass field, my friend Jerry Driskell started to crouch down and move ever so slowly towards a brown spot in the grass. He reached down and grabbed a rabbit from the grass. It kicked and pulled itself out of Jerry's grasp. I was amazed and thought rabbits would be easy. I was wrong. Never saw another sit still like that again.

At home chores began. My assignment was chopping wood for the stove. Oh, right about that stove. As I mentioned earlier our little house had two bedrooms. Mom and Dad were in one with Krissy. Candy and Chery had the other. So. I was left with a small bed in one corner of the living room behind the couch and the wood stove. While most folks in the area heated their homes with fireplaces and potbellied stoves, we didn't have a fireplace. Dad bought this designer wood stove that had a small firebox. It was supposed to be super-efficient. It wasn't, the wood hardly burned and it gave off little heat. I would put bricks on top of the stove, wrap them in a towel and place them at the foot of my bed. Next to my bed was a little mahogany stained desk that Mom designated as my "chest of drawers". We had a propane tank and the kitchen stove and water heater used that fuel. Every now and then Dad would light the oven and leave the oven door open just to get some heat in the kitchen. I would drag my blanket and pillow to the kitchen and try to get warm enough to go to sleep. Later on, Dad installed a gas wall furnace in the hallway. More about that later.

Jerry Birdsong was one of the tallest eighth grade boys. As it turned out, Jerry had two younger brothers, Jarrett and Jerald. They lived on C highway, about a mile from our farm. Jerry, his brothers and I would go squirrel hunting with the help of their super squirrel dog, Bullet. I think Jerry's dad was a rural postman. I remember his mom being one of sweetest persons I ever met and she was beautiful to boot. She and my mom were good friends. The Birdsongs lived on the south side of C Highway just outside town. The next house closer to town was the home of Paul Roy and his wife Gerry, the owners of the only gas station and dry goods store in the area.

The closest farmhouse to ours was the home of Sonny Hodgson. I think he was related to the Hodgson Mill folks or so he said. I remember visiting his house once. They didn't have running water. You drew water from the well that was located in the house. It had a long skinny cylindrical bucket and a rope over a pulley or sheave. You lowered the bucket down the well, a valve on the bottom would open, the bucket would fill, the valve would close when you pulled up the bucket.

Sonny had an outhouse. Next to the toilet seat was a Sears Roebuck catalog. It wasn't for shopping.

I went on one criminal enterprise with Sonny. We sneaked into a farmer's field and rode two of his work horses bareback all over the pasture. We used rope hackamores to guide the gentle beasts. It was great fun and, as far as I know, no one ever found out about it.

CHAPTER 7. HUNTING AND FISHING COUNTRY STYLE

My Dad gave me a 22 single-shot JC Higgins rifle for my birthday when I was nine in Alameda California. I remember being taught all the Marine sniper firing positions. Dad was always pushing my butt down. "You don't want to get it shot off, do you?" It helped on the Dora farm with rabbits, squirrels and bullfrogs. I would hunt squirrels with the Birdsong Boys and on my own. I remember chasing a squirrel down a gravel road just north of the farm. I shot and missed several times at this rascal. When I got home, Dad was waiting to discuss the rounds he heard going through the tree leaves just above where my baby sister Krissy was playing. Lesson learned.

I loved to hunt bullfrogs. At first, I would shoot the frogs on the bank or just in the water. I aimed at the frog's head but it wasn't perfect. Later on I discovered the 22 long rifle hollow point rounds would stun the frog in the water without actually hitting the frog. I would just wade in water, retrieve the frog and dispatch him with a blow to the head. It made dressing the frog less messy and more efficient. I filled the freezer with frog legs, rabbit, squirrel, and pond perch. The perch were thick in the big pond and grasshoppers were readily available. But, sometimes I didn't even need fresh bait. The perch were so hungry they would bite an empty hook.

The 22 was handy for dispatching possums, skunks and ground hogs that were becoming nuisances. But, Tripoli was the better hunter and varmint dispatcher.

Now about that 22. It didn't have a proper front sight. The little round bead that was supposed to sit on top of the blade was missing. So, Dad, in his wisdom, trained me to use the front blade like a military rifle. That worked fine for distance shots but up close it would shoot very high. It was irritating. There was this possum that kept raiding the chicken nests for eggs. I shot at him three times at about 20 ft. Never hit him. Dad was watching, not being critical, just laughing. He knew what the problem was, just waiting for me to figure it out.

There were other problems with the 22. It would misfire every 10 rounds. That was a real problem for a single shot rifle. But, I learned to cope.

I caught nothing but perch from the big pond. But once Dad caught a huge carp and brought it up to the house to show off. He filled the bathtub and put the carp in the water. Then he grabbed Thai, the Siamese, and held him over the water so he could see it. To this day we still talk about that cat saying Wow! He really did. But there are other stories about Dad teasing the cats.

Once Dad caught a black snake in the front yard. It was harmless. He let it wrap around his arm and let Chery touch the squirming reptile. Then he put the large snake on the ground and grabbed Inky, the black and white cat. He said "watch this", held Inky over the snake and let him drop. In defiance of the laws of physics, the cat moved sideways in the air and hit the ground 3 feet away from the coiled snake. Amazing.

CHAPTER 8. THE FIRST WINTER

South Missouri is not like California or North Carolina. Winters get cold. The farm house was set on a hill above the milking barn and a small pond in the barnyard that the livestock would use. It had gold fish that would follow you around the banks of the pond.

The first blast of winter came as a freezing rain. I woke up in the morning to a quarter inch thick, crystal-clear coating of ice on everything. It was beautiful. The bush and tree branches were bowed over under the weight. The leaves that had hung on through the fall were delicately encased. The ground looked like brown pottery with a glass coating. I maneuvered down the slick steps and stepped on the ground. The slope took over and I was on my way to the barnyard pond. Luckily, I was able to grab the front yard gatepost and arrest the slide. I then crawled back to the front steps on all fours.

It stayed very cold for several weeks. The ponds froze solid. The ice was over 3 inches thick and you could walk on the ice with little danger. I would slide around on the ice of the barnyard pond and watch the gold fish under the ice follow me around. I chopped through the ice with an ax so the cows could drink then threw some grain in the water. The goldfish became a pack of piranhas. As our Siamese cat, Thai, would say "Wow".

Having one of the only flowing water systems in the area meant freezing problems in the coldest days. Dad would try every day to keep the well house above freezing and only lost the battle a couple of times.

Dad installed a vent-less, gas wall heater in the hallway that connected the bedrooms. When it got so cold in the house we couldn't stand it, we would go in the hallway and close the bedroom doors so all the heat stayed in the hallway. It was great but probably cost us a few brain cells. Vent-less in 1957 meant "sort of vent-less".

CHAPTER 9. SPRING AT LAST

It was a cold, long winter. There was a round of flu going through the school and I got very ill. But Spring started and the sun shone. Even before the buds came out Dad put my bed out on the porch in the sunlight. Something about needing Vitamin D as I recall. I recovered quickly. The flu epidemic over, it was now 7th Grade Softball season and maybe some school work.

At the farm, it was Bambi and Thumper time. Dad took me out to the southeast pasture to watch a calf be born. It was beautiful and stomach turning at the same time.

That was just one part of the equation. Later on, I witnessed the Vet artificially inseminate a cow. A long rubber glove and a glass vile out of the cooler. Then came the poor ordeal for Inky and Thai, the two cats. One at a time their upper bodies were placed in a pants leg headfirst with just their lower legs exposed. Then Dad had me hold the cat's legs while he took a razor blade and neutered the poor animal. Weird to a 13 year old. I guess I was supposed to figure it all out from there. So much for Dad's "Birds and the Bees" talk.

The buds and flowers began. There were more calves and then piglets. We had to build a special crate so the sows wouldn't roll over on their newborn. The piglets were fun though. But they wouldn't stay cute.

One of the first calves was all light brown. Dad named her Fawn. Unfortunately, she came down with scours and stayed weak. I'll never forget the day. Dad just walked Fawn up to the old abandoned well with his 38 caliber revolver in his hand. At the well he shot her in the head and pushed her into the well. He went to the barn and got a sack of lime, then poured it in the well. There were tears in his eyes, the old Marine softy.

Dad put me in charge of an Angus calf. It was fun until it was time for him to go to market. Dad just put a rope around the now large calf and used the Cub to drag him to the cattle truck. Later on, the freezer was stocked with beef. I never put that all together. That happened in the Fall of 1957 so let's back up to the Spring again.

The rains came. Little rivers formed and flowed from the farm to the pond. My sisters and I would dam up the little rivers. We made miniature waterfalls with three dams. We named the dams, Damn, Darn and Dern. Leaves became boats and sailed down the little rivers and over the waterfalls. It was great fun but didn't get chores done.

Rain makes lawn grass and field oats grow. And grass must be mowed in the yard and oats must be cut in the field. The Farmall Cub had a sling mower arm and was used for the oats. An unreliable Sears Craftsman 2 stroke mower was used for the lawn. I hated that mower. But it was better than the old manual roller mower which was useless for Missouri grass. I always had trouble starting the Craftsman. You had to rewind the starter cord after each pull. There were no recoil starters in those days. I pulled the cord enough to mow the whole yard without using any gas.

CHAPTER 10. MISSOURI SUMMERS ARE HOT

After a wet Spring came a very dry early summer. The early oats were cut, raked and baled. Dad connected a heavy wooden wagon to the Cub and we started picking up the oat bales and stacking them on the wagon. The bales were tied with cord, not wire. You could horse them around without gloves, or so Dad thought. But my hands were not as tough as Dad's. It hurt but then the blisters turned to calluses. All was right with the World.

Hauling the hay to the barn should have been easy. But my nemesis, the barnyard pond, nearly got me again. I pulled the trailer up towards the farmhouse in order to back towards the barn. I hadn't quite straightened out the trailer and Cub when the Cub ran out of gas. The angle had the trailer pointed at the pond. No matter how hard I pushed on the brakes, the whole rig started creeping towards the pond. At first, I panicked. I was still in first gear but we were still moving. Then I had a flash of brilliance. I turned the Cub and jackknifed the trailer. I got some gas and started the Cub. My plan worked but I never told Dad. I should have. The next day he was the solo driver. The tractor stalled going up the hill and wouldn't start. It rolled back to the muddy edge of the pond. We had to winch the trailer out of the mud. I felt a little guilty but also a bit amused. The smartest man I would ever know wasn't perfect.

As the oldest sibling and a boy, I was the de facto leader. My sisters and I played Wagon Train and hooked up Tripoli to Krissy's stroller. She would pull Krissy all the way to the Big Pond. We would throw old blankets over the bushes to create a makeshift tent. Then we discovered chiggers. No more "Happy Trails" adventures after that.

Mom loved to swim in the Big Pond. One day she invited Mrs. Birdsong and her boys over a dip in the pond. Now my sisters were still pretty young and Mom thought nothing about them running around bare chested. There we were with Mrs. Birdsong and her boys when my sisters came running out to swim. The Birdsong boys smirked and I died. I had a long discussion with Mom after that. And that was that. No more aborigines on the Capages Farm.

In late Summer we were busy. Dad was milking 15 cows including a mixed Angus and Holstein cow named Black Mamba. We were a Grade C dairy, so the milk was mostly used for making cheese. I still remember Dad holding onto Black Mamba's tail as she dragged him through the milking barn. You had to be there.

CHAPTER 11. TENNESSEE DETOUR

In late Summer, something changed. Dad sold all the stock and the Farmall Cub. We suddenly packed up the whole family and moved in with my Mom's mother in Millington Tennessee. I think Mom and Dad had concluded that we wouldn't survive the winter financially. Dad winterized the equipment and the farm house and we moved in with Granny Downstairs in Tennessee. My Mom's mother was Mrs. Mary Powell. To keep things simple, we called Dad's mom Granny Upstairs. Her real name was Mrs. Mary Capages of course. She lived on the fourth floor of an apartment in New York City, get it?

I spent the first half of the eighth grade in Millington. There was Sputnik and Ozzie and Harriet. The eighth grade girls started filling out. We boys noticed. One girl did a modern dance interpretation to Bee-Bop-a-Lua. She was in black leotards. It was a scandal but we boys loved it.

Times were tough. Dad sold encyclopedias door to door to make a living. Someone poisoned Tripoli and she got very sick. I stayed with her continually, stroking her neck and whispering in her ear. My uncle, Doc Hall, was a veterinarian. He looked Tripoli over and I heard him tell Dad it was probably strychnine. There was no hope. That night Dad bundled up Tripoli and left. I never saw my sweet protector again. I hated Millington Tennessee.

CHAPTER 12. BACK TO DORA

In February 1958, we returned to the Farm. Everything was as we left it. The chickens that had survived had multiplied with one exception. Dad found a chicken carcass on an old bed of coals. As it turned out, some of the local boys had raided the chicken house and tried to cook a chicken. They didn't know to pluck the feathers first. It must have smelled awful. Dad would still chuckle about it years later.

There was no real Farm income now. We picked blackberries and sold them to people driving by on C Highway. We also picked up black walnuts and dehulled them using a contraption that consisted of a wooden trough and the back wheel of the car. When the wheel turned the walnuts were poured into the trough and the hulls were scrubbed off by the rotating tire. The dehulled walnuts were put in burlap feed sacks and sold for $10 a sack, or maybe it was $3, I forget. Our fingers and hands turned green. Most of the farm kids had green fingers so it was a kind of badge of honor at school.

Dad had always been an archery aficionado and was quite talented in making composite bows when he had spare time. On the farm, he had no spare time. He even had to sell some of his most beautiful bows. One went to Preacher Roe in West Plains.

It still wasn't enough to survive so Dad went to Springfield Missouri and got a job in the Sears repair shop. He mostly repaired lawn mowers. Then he traded in the 56 Plymouth station wagon for an old black 46 Chevy coupe. We needed the cash difference. He would drive that old Chevy 90 miles to Springfield every day and return in late evening. The roads were winding and up and down two-lane highways. On one trip, a tie rod failed and Dad nearly crashed. The hardened Marine officer had a little chat with the car dealer. He made it good.

Dad was now making more money in Springfield than the farm could produce. And he had moved up the ranks in the Sears Repair Shop.

It seemed everything came from Sears. I finally got some "Ivy League" shirts and slacks by mail order from Sears, a surprise gift from Mom. The shirts had vertical stripes and box pleats on the backs. The slacks had a buckle on the back. These were the "in thing" in Millington but we couldn't afford them then. They didn't mean much in Dora. Button fly Levi's were the fashion, even for the girls. Now here comes the Sears kid with some dumb looking jeans with curved flaps on the front pockets. Dad got me those and I hated them. I would turn the pocket flaps in so they looked like Levi's. I finally got some Levi's from Paul Roy's store.

CHAPTER 13. RETURN TO WINDELL HALL'S EIGHTH GRADE CLASS

It was as if I had never left. Now I was in Windell Hall's eighth grade class and there was a new crop of seventh graders. Windell had his hands full with one kid, Jesse Croney. One time he grabbed Jesse by both collars and held him up against the wall to get his attention. He got it. I think it was a "failure to communicate" since Jesse would turn out to be a good kid. There were some cute seventh grade girls. Geraldine Hambelton and Claudia Johnson come to mind. But too young for eighth grade boys at the time.

It was softball season again and I was still making good grades. Unfortunately, the grades were too good. At graduation, I would be Valedictorian and Windell had plans. He handed me a full page of single spaced text to memorize. The one phrase in the speech was the German "Auf Wiedersehen" or "till we meet again". I struggled with that until I changed my crib sheet to "off veederzane". To me it went off went off without a hitch. But Dad would sometimes smile about the speech as though he had some secret. You see, during the first part of my speech, a young girl started walking down the aisle. I think it was one of my classmates, Dottie Dobbs. From the podium, I waved at her and told her to sit down. She sat down immediately in the lap of a stranger two rows in front of her own dad. The audience laughed when she jumped up and ran back to her seat next to her dad. Dad said I had command presence but needed to work on giving clearer instructions. Very funny.

In early summer, I would ride my bike over to Bob Barlow's house. His family car had a great radio and we would listen to Elvis and Paul Anka. But then there was Purple People Eater, we knew every line. Bob's mom would eventually be my Freshman English Teacher. She was one smart lady.

There was a little café in Dora, just north after the curve past Bob Barlow's. I remember seeing my first 1958 Chevy Impala parked in front of that café. It was black with a red interior with twin radio antennas on the rear fenders. The car had dual headlights, the first of its kind I think. The sounds of Old Lonesome Me by Don Gibson and Many a Tear Has to Fall by Jim Reeves came floating out of the café. Another schoolmate of mine, Kenny Kutter, lived across the street from that café. But it was his older sister, Karen, that caught all our attention. She was gorgeous. The older guys just fluttered around her.

CHAPTER 14. I GET WHEELS.

Dad's work at the Sears repair shop had other advantages. Dad brought home a better lawn mower. Then he got the idea to use the old mower's engine to motorize my bicycle. He started working on it every night when he got home. At Sears, he ordered a large pulley that fastened to the rear wheel.

Then he mounted the Craftsman 2 stroke engine to the frame and brazed an idler pulley to the seat tube. The crazy contraption ran great. No more starter cord to pull. I would just start peddling and the now "motorbike" would come to life. Now I loved that old two-stroke. It would even run on white gas from Paul Roy's station. Much cheaper.

The exhaust pipe was very short and would blow hot exhaust on my left inner thigh. I solved that problem when I found a used chrome-plated P-trap left over from the kitchen remodeling. It slipped over the engine exhaust and directed the exhaust to the rear. It looked as though it was made for it. At first, I controlled the speed with a string attached to the throttle bell crank. Later on, I used an old 10 speed bike brake lever to control the throttle, from the Sears junk pile of course. For my birthday, I got a battery operated front headlight. The motorbike was complete and I rode it everywhere. One day I was filling the little engine's gas tank at Roy's and Kelly Martin drove up in his family's pickup. He asked to take the bike for a spin. I agreed with some trepidation. But he rode it up and down the gravel road just fine. Kelly said it was a "remarkable invention" but needed a back seat for his girlfriend. He would have needed three back seats at the time as I recall.

When I left the station that day I stopped at the Birdsong's. Jerry was in trouble because he had flipped the family Pontiac into the ditch on the curve of C Highway just before their house. His dad was furious with him and he was grounded. A couple weeks later I slid my motorbike off the road at the same place when my headlight stopped working. Nothing damaged but my pride. You don't get grounded if no one knows about it.

CHAPTER 15. A DORA FRESHMAN

Now, with Dad traveling to Springfield every day, I was responsible for most of the heavy chores. I whitewashed buildings, even the bases of some trees. I thought the place looked like Tara from "Gone with the Wind". The new lawn mower helped around the house but now I had to cut the tall weeds outside the yard with a sling blade. It was never ending but I still managed to practice shooting baskets in the back yard. But there were issues with that. The basketball goal was attached to the rear of the house and there was a pile of bricks just behind me. The chickens left little land mines all over the place. I would shoot and try to catch the ball before it hit the ground. If I missed the rebound I would have to wipe the chicken poop off the ball. It forced me to follow my shots, a good thing. If the ball hit the brick pile, it would rebound off in unpredictable directions but always into a pile of chicken poop. To practice dribbling I had to bounce twice and wipe once.

Once Krissy was sitting there watching my practice shots. Candy came out to watch as well. She picked a loose brick up off the ground and tried to toss it onto the brick pile. The brick hit Krissy flat on the forehead. Later on Chery would say I tossed the brick. She wasn't there so I wonder the source of that version of the event. Candy would eventually confess.

Week end entertainment was the Dora Skating Rink. It was a larger Quonset hut style building and was the social center. Preparation required ironing my starched Levi's to get a knife edge crease and splashing on Dad's Old Spice. It's what you did. The eighth graders would race and slide around the corners. But the high school girls would skate with their boyfriends to the Everly Brothers' "All I Have To Do Is Dream" and all of Pat Boone's latest. It was sort of a gliding waltz with Virginia and Scharlotte Martin in their element. Beautiful to watch.

Photos courtesy of Mary Collins-Dora School Library

I was a bit unfortunate. Ronnie Thornton and Don Collins had rubber toe stops on their skates. They could start and stop on a dime. All I could do was slide to a stop. I was always replacing or truing up the flat wooden skate wheels. The rink entry fee was a quarter, inexpensive social entertainment. There were never any fights or negative events, which was notable since the Dora Baseball team had hair triggers when players from the other local teams dropped in.

One day five of us went for a ride in a 1957 Oldsmobile. It had pillars down the back window and made a statement. The driver was Ronnie Thornton, age 14. We went north from the Skating Rink up the two-lane highway. We hit 100 miles per hour. Then we slowed down and Ronnie stopped after we crossed a pneumatic hose the County had placed across the road to measure the traffic flow. Someone decided to get out of the car and jump up and down on the hose, reason unknown. In the distance, we saw a car coming so we jumped back in the car and Ronnie whipped us into a side road behind some trees. The car went by. It was the Highway Patrol. He never saw us. Ronnie pulled out a cigarette and lit it. As the waves of smoke hit the back seat, my nerves settled. I have never smoked a cigarette to this day, but I get it. It helped me understand Dad a little better. He had been in combat in Okinawa and Korea.[1] He smoked two packs a day most of his life.

---

[1] See *THE SILENT SECOND: The Biography of Martin Capages-Captain USMC*-available at Amazon.com

CHAPTER 16. LEARNING HOW NOT TO GAMBLE

Another social event was the Dora Carnival or the Dora Picnic. It was not a school event. It was fun, cotton candy, bumper cars and carnies. The carnies had a "spin the wheel" game and I had four quarters. I bet a quarter and spun the wheel. I won a dime plus my quarter. I went again with the same results. I made it to a profit of 50 cents then my luck changed. I kept losing until I got down to my last two quarters. I figured out the wheel was rigged. I needed my quarters for the Skating Rink and a Coke. The lesson was learned. Quit when you're ahead or don't gamble at all, preferably the latter.

CHAPTER 17. BASKETBALL

High Schoolers didn't play softball. It was hard ball and not for Freshman because I don't remember being on a Freshman hardball team. The school had changed in other ways too. We now had a new gymnasium and a new basketball coach, Paul Batesel, fresh out of college. It was his first teaching and coaching job. He taught Freshman math and coached the Varsity and B Team basketball squads. At Millington, I had learned to dribble and shoot layups. Not even the Seniors had done that in a gymnasium with wood floors. As a freshman, I played on the B Team and Varsity. The freshman and sophomores played on the B Team. Three sophomores played on the Varsity, my two friends Kelly Martin and Jerry Birdsong. The other sophomore was new to me. His name was Sonny DeBoard. He was the best all around player on the team and I copied every move he made.

Our best set shooter was John Hamby. He rarely missed a shot. John had a unique, unorthodox style that drove Coach Batesel to distraction. But, Sonny was a crazy man dribbling. He would imitate the Harlem Globe Trotters. His layup shots were incredible. I concentrated on jump shots and modeled my style after the pros and a kid who played for Bakersfield. Bakersfield trounced our Varsity and B Team. I played in both games but only touched the ball twice in the Varsity game. Missed a layup and hit a jump shot. It was enough to earn a Varsity letter as a Freshman.

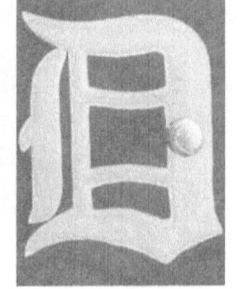

Sonny DeBoard had all the gear. He even had a gym bag. I had to carry my basketball shoes, warmups and game uniform in a brown paper bag. Not very professional but effective. I was usually the youngest in class because my birthday was in late August. It didn't hurt my grades but there were some unfounded worries about showering with the more mature male team mates. But puberty took over and hair grew on my upper lip and elsewhere just in time.

Coach Batesel was only a couple years older than some of the senior cheerleaders. It was a good thing the school colors were red and white. But he often had lipstick on his collar after the away games anyway. I remember who the young lady was, but I'm not telling. I admired Coach Batesel and thought he did a good job as a rookie.

This photo from the 1959 Doramo yearbook, posted on the Dora School Library Facebook page, shows the DHS basketball A and B teams during one of the years Martin Capages and his friends participated. From left: John Hamby, Kelly Martin, Sonny DeBoard, Jerry Birdsong, Martin Capages, Larry Owen, Teddy Thornton, Don Nielson, Don Driskell, Jim Shipley and coach Paul Batesel.

CHAPTER 18. GYPSIES AGAIN

As a freshman, my girlfriend was Linda Stout, an eighth grader. We never even held hands. But we did wear these pins that said we were going steady. We never even had a date or even kissed. I'm not sure what going steady meant in those days. Seemed to be expensive.

After Christmas 1958, Dad broke the news. We were moving to Springfield so Dad would be closer to work. He was now a full time Sears Repairman and would soon be the Shop supervisor. To me, it was the end of the World. Dad borrowed a Sears delivery truck, we loaded it up with all our furniture and appliances. With four kids in the back sitting on mattresses, we left the Dora Farm for good. That kept my record intact. I never attended any school more than one year until I walked into Parkview High School in January 1959. Time to start over. Linda Stout sent me my pin back and I mailed her hers. I think she started dating Kelly Martin. I could be wrong.

YEAR BOOK PHOTOS
Courtesy Mary Collins and the Dora School Library

This photo of the Dora Grade School basketball team is from the 1957 *Doramo* yearbook, published by the Dora High School "annual" staff and shared on the Dora School Library Facebook page. Front row, from left: John Moritz, Kelly Martin, Jerry Barcus, Gary Decker and Stanley Adams (partially hidden). Middle: Martin Capages, Robby Hollingshad and Teddy Thornton. Back: Tommy Shipley, Jerry Warren, Bob Barlow and Sonny Hodgson.

OZARK COUNTY HEART
Boyhood Memories of a Dora Missouri Farm

1957 YEAR BOOK

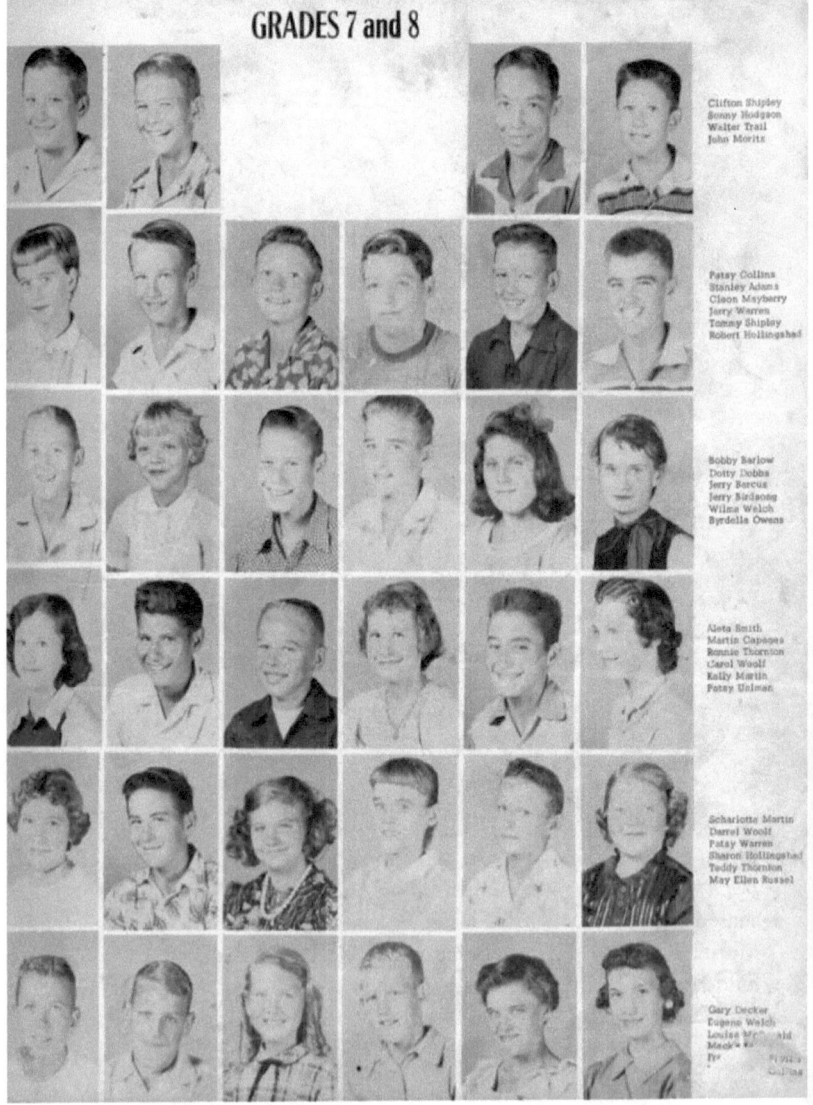

GRADES 7 and 8

Clifton Shipley
Sonny Hudgson
Walter Trail
John Moritz

Patsy Collins
Stanley Adams
Cleon Mayberry
Jerry Warren
Tommy Shipley
Robert Hollingshad

Bobby Barlow
Dotty Dobbs
Jerry Borcux
Jerry Sizdoong
Wilma Welch
Byrdella Owens

Aleta Smith
Martin Capsoes
Ronnie Thornton
Carol Woolf
Kelly Martin
Patsy Uniman

Scharlotte Martin
Darrel Woolf
Patsy Warren
Sharon Hollingshad
Teddy Thornton
May Ellen Russel

Gary Decker
Eugene Welch
Louise McDonald
Mack's ...

OZARK COUNTY HEART
Boyhood Memories of a Dora Missouri Farm

OZARK COUNTY HEART
Boyhood Memories of a Dora Missouri Farm

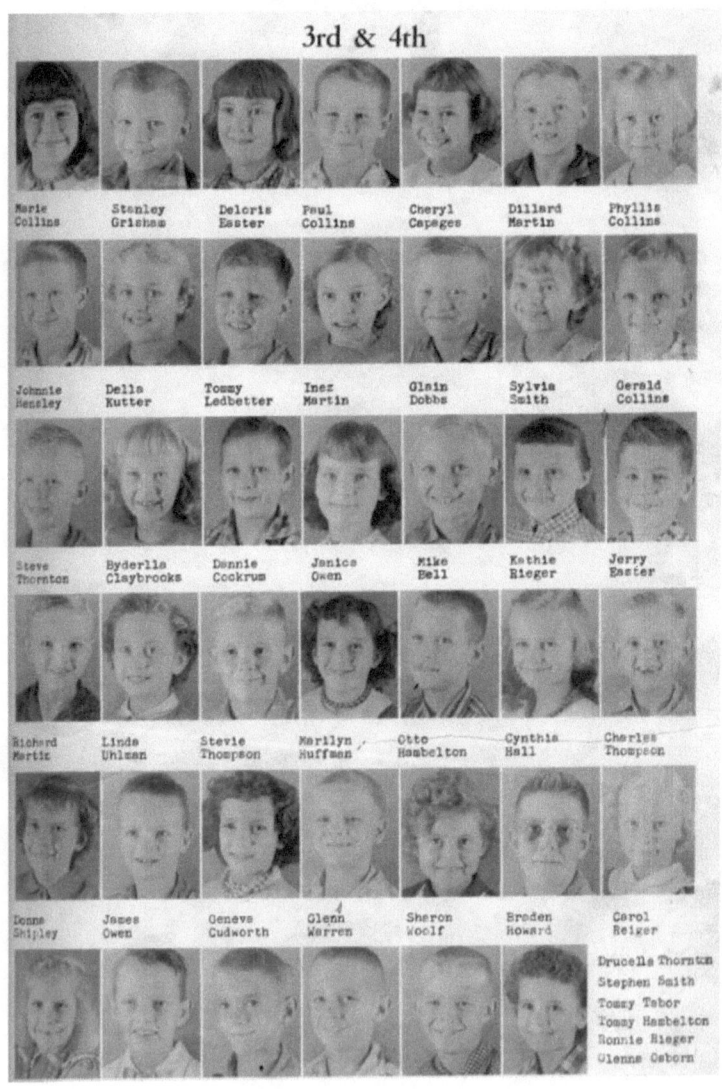

OZARK COUNTY HEART
Boyhood Memories of a Dora Missouri Farm

1958 YEARBOOK

7th & 8th

Sandra Smith	Thomas Shipley	Geraldine Hambelton	Radis Smith	Juanita Cudworth	Kenny Kutter	Lula Jean Collins
Wayne Hodgson	Carol Woolf	Leroy Collins	Dottie Dobbs	Ronnie Decker	Patsy Uhlsann	Don Collins
Joe Dickison	Jarrett Birdsong	Troy Johnson	Phillip Moritz	Guy Tucker	Lyle Thornton	Jerry Welton
Byrdella Owens	John Nash	Louise McDonald	James Hollingshed	Lawana Easter	Doyne Elliot	Claudia Johnson
Mackie Welch	Patsy Warren	Clifton Shipley	Clifford Hensley	Ronnie Thornton	Bobby Berlow	Danny Ziegler

Jerry Johnson
Jesse Croney
John Spangler
Billy Leroy
Martin Capages

OZARK COUNTY HEART
Boyhood Memories of a Dora Missouri Farm

1959 YEARBOOK

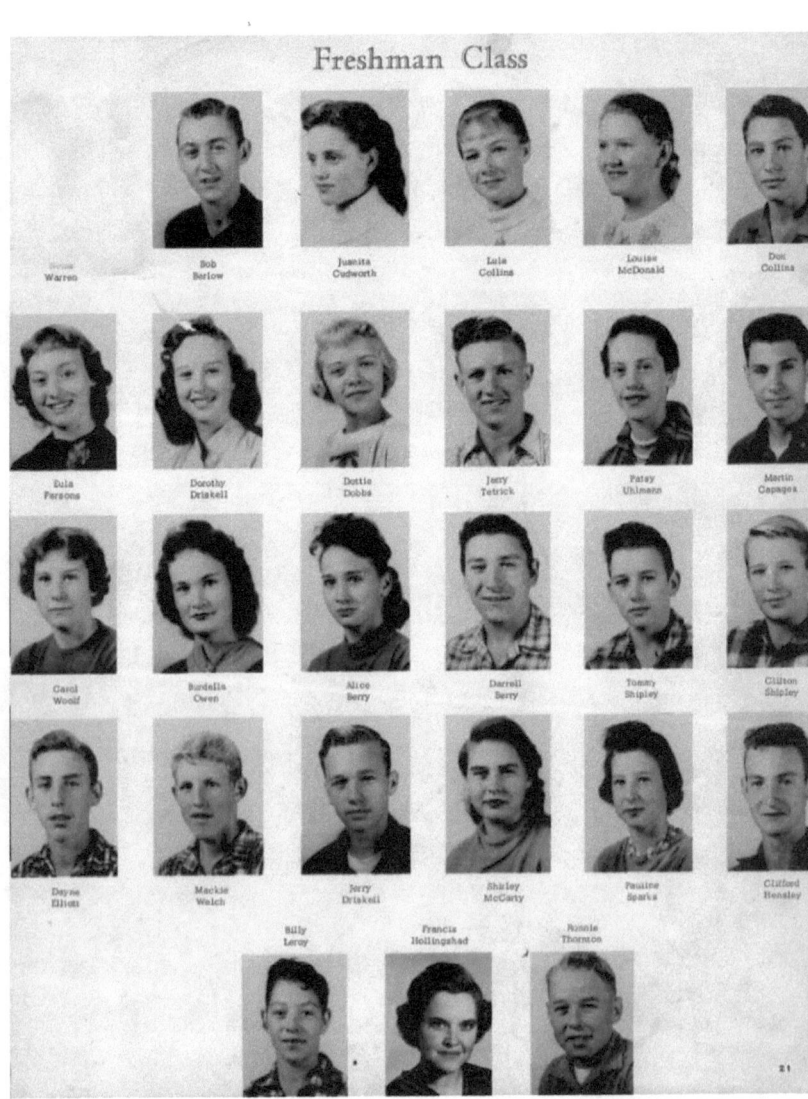

FIFTY YEARS LATER

The 50th year reunion of that first Dora high school basketball team was one of the most memorable times in my life. Most of the success was attributable to Virginia Martin Berry, President of the 1959 Dora graduating class, the 2008-9 Falcon coaching staff, school administration and local graduates. But I especially want to thank Norene Prososki and Sue Ann Jones of the Ozark County Times who made the 2009 event even more special with their coverage of the reunion.

In 2008, Coach Batesel sent the following letter to me that I forwarded to the Ozark County Times for that special reunion of the 1958 Dora Falcons first basketball team in February 2009:

"Dear Dora Falcons:

I was in the neighborhood in September for my niece's wedding in Mammoth. I drove by the old Gainesville school where Dora played its first game. I'll never forget how small that gym was, how none of us had a clue as to what we were doing and how badly they beat us. The gym doesn't look any larger today.

I remember that our own gym wasn't finished when school started and that we practiced on an outside goal east of the school. When the floor was finished the players painted the lines, and Mrs. Barlow painted the old English D in the center circle. A few days later the floor swelled and buckled. We had to have strips cut out of it to give it space to settle back down. I also remember that before the Koshkonong game the cheerleaders spent the day mopping and waxing the floor. The first player to try to change directions that night is probably still flying in space.

We took some really bad beatings that year, but almost won the homecoming game against Birch Tree. No one on the team had any playing experience, but it was a neat group of people who deserved better. What can I tell you? I was just twenty years old—only a couple of years older than some of the Seniors—and I didn't have the maturity or expertise to help the team improve. I regret that a great deal. If life awarded do-overs, I would like to try that year with you again. I look at the names and pictures, and they bring back good memories. Fifty years is a long time, and it's good to see that so many players and cheerleaders are still with us. I appreciate Martin's effort to get everyone back together, and I would really like to see you all again. But in North Dakota in February, even getting out of a driveway is iffy.
Best Wishes to all
Paul Batesel"

PAUL BATESEL
S. M. S. Springfield
Sophomore Sponsor
Coach
Math, Physical Education

OZARK COUNTY HEART
Boyhood Memories of a Dora Missouri Farm

REUNION

The following is the reporting done by Sue Ann Jones of the Ozark County Times in the build-up to the Dora Class of 1959 and the First Basketball Team Reunion on February 18, 2009. [Sue Ann Luna Jones sueann@ozarkcountytimes.com]

Something really special is being planned for Friday night at Dora High School, when the rural community will gather to celebrate homecoming and watch the girls' and boys' basketball games.
In addition to crowning the homecoming king and queen, and besides observing the DHS homecoming tradition of welcoming back alumni who graduated 20 years ago, the school also will honor the students who started Dora's basketball program 50 years ago.

Local News

Dora School's First Basketball Team Remembers And Celebrates Early Days

Email this article
Printer friendly page

Members of Dora High School's first basketball team who gathered Friday night at the school for a 50-year reunion included, from left, Lonnie Johnson, Kelly Martin, Jerry Birdsong, Larry Owen, Martin Capages, Don Nielsen, Teddy Thornton, John Moritz, Wayne Marshall and Jimmy Shipley.

When members of Dora High School's first basketball team and cheerleading squad were honored Friday during the school's homecoming activities, one of the special memories shared was Jimmy Shipley's story of playing basketball as a seventh-grader at Dora, before the school had a gymnasium.

"We played outside on a dirt court," he said. When the team was invited to play in a junior high tournament in Gainesville, the boys stepped out on the gym floor just like they played back at Dora, "wearing our boots and work shoes," Jimmy said. When officials refused to let them play in their boots, the boys sat down to take off their shoes and play barefooted. But that too was prohibited.

"So one of the Gainesville coaches went into the locker room and found us some of his boys' shoes to wear, and that's how we got to play," Shipley said. The problem ended there. "We lost the first game, so we didn't have to play any more."

© Copyright 2008 by www.ozarkcountytimes.com

More than a dozen of the original team members and cheerleaders are expected to attend, said organizer Martin Capages. Even though he was only a freshman during the 1958-1959 school year, when the program began, he was allowed to play on the varsity team. And he considered the team's upperclassmen his heroes, he said.

Two of those upperclassmen were the first team's co-captains, Don Nielsen and Larry Owen, who plan to attend the Friday event. Now, 50 years later, they laugh remembering that first winless season. "I guess we just weren't too smart, us Dora boys," said Neilsen, a Pomona dairy farmer for 45 years. "None of us had ever played basketball. And Coach[Paul] Batesel was just 19 or 20 years old. He didn't know much more about it than we did. But we just kept thinking we could win."

And once during that first season, the Dora Falcons almost did in.

"We had played Winona early in the season, and they beat us pretty bad, something like 70 to 40. But we got better as the season went on. When Winona came to Dora near the end of the season, they beat us by just two points – in overtime," said Nielsen, who blames himself for the loss. "I stole the ball and then missed the layup," he said.

Another memorable game occurred during the West Plains Invitational Tournament.

"A little ol' 1A team like us shouldn't have even been in that tournament," Nielsen said. "But back then, it didn't matter what size school you were, everyone played in the tournaments. We played the West Plains B team, and they beat us 125 to 25. The next day on the radio, the announcer was reading off the scores, and when he read that one, he said, 'I don't know. That doesn't sound right. I'll have to check on that.' But it was right. They really stomped us."

But the Dora Falcons weren't discouraged. They just kept right on going. 'And besides, there was something neat about that game,"

Nielsen said. "I was a big baseball fan, and Bill Virdon, a West Plains boy who had played professional baseball, refereed our game against the West Plains B team. I thought that was something - even though we couldn't even get the ball past the center line against that team."

As he recalls, the West Plains B team went onto win the tournament, beating West Plains own A team. and later, as West Plains varsity, won the state championship.

B team member Jerry Birdsong, now retired on an Ozark County farm after living in Los Angeles for more than 30 years, remembers the West Plains A team that year was coached by the late Jim Peters. The West Plains B team was coached by Jim Smoot, now a State Farm insurance agent in St. James. Smoot confirmed the 100-point victory. "l ran in every player I could out there, but that's what happened against that Dora team," he said.

Smoot also recalled that he had refereed one of the first basketball games at Dora. 'They didn't have a time clock yet, and they kept time with an alarm clock," he said. "That game nearly went on all night."

Player Kelly Martin remembers that the best player on the West Plains team was Gary Garner, who went on to star for Mizzou and become a college coach.

Nielsen added that Dora's first basketball team might not have been a powerhouse, "but it was a different story when it came to baseball. Then West Plains didn't want to see us coming, because we had a really good baseball team that could beat just about anybody."

John Moritz, another Dora B team player. remembers that the "B team just won one game during my three years there. We weren't the best in the world, but we had fun doing it."

Some of Dora's first basketball team members had never touched a basketball before the team was organized. Others, ,like Larry Owen, had played a little ball in grade school, before Dora reorganized into a consolidated district and built a new two-story high school addition, which also included the school's first gym. That structure burned in a devastating fire 11 years ago that destroyed most of the school, which was quickly rebuilt.

"In grade school, before they built the gym, we played on a dirt court," said Owen, a minister who has worked all around the country and now lives in Pocahontas, Ark. "We couldn't dribble because sometimes the ground was soft. But we could pass and shoot," he said.

Batesel, the team's first coach, lives in North Dakota and won't be able to attend Friday's reunion. But he sent a letter reminiscing about the team's experiences. Remembering the Falcons' first away game, in the Gainesville gym that's now the local post office building, he wrote, "I'll never forget how small that gym was, how none of us had a clue as to what we were doing and how badly they beat us."

Dora's own gym wasn't quite completed when the 1958-1959 school year began, Batesel recalled. "When it was finished, the players painted the lines, and Mrs. Barlow painted the old English D in the center circle. A few days later the floor swelled and buckled. We had to have strips cut out of it to give it space to settle back down," he wrote. "I also remember that before the Koshkonong game the cheerleaders spent the day mopping and waxing the floor. The first player to try to change directions that night is probably still flying in space."

Reading Coach Batesel's letter, Dora faculty member Marcie Roberts said she found it ironic that the first team chose the old English D because, without knowing that fact, this year's students were "adamant" about using the old English font on this year's homecoming T-shirt.

Several players remember that Sonny DeBoard, a West Plains resident who attended DHS because his dad taught there, as the best dribbler on the team. He was also the shortest, maybe just 5'6" or so, said the

6'2' Owen, who laughed, remembering that he and DeBoard played guard and center.

DeBoard is one of two members of Dora's first team that have not been located by the reunion organizers. The other is Wayne Marshall. [Wayne Marshall did attend the reunion]

Team member Kelly Martin remembers that the Falcons' first win came during its second year. "We beat Koshkonong, something like 48 to 44," he said, recalling that the team always played in front of a good home crowd. "The community supported us," he said.

Capages, a PhD, University Missouri-Rolla graduate and owner of ARIS Engineering in Springfield, moved away from Dora after his freshman year, but the memory of being part the fledgling basketball are special to him, especially since he got to play varsity. "Those guys were my heroes," he said. "It was such an honor for me, a little freshman, to get to play with them on that team."

Dora had cheerleaders for the first time during the basketball team's first year. One of them, Delores Shipley Barlow now living in Guthrie, Okla., remembers the girls wore plain white turtleneck sweaters and long red-corduroy circle skirts they made themselves We really enjoyed all of it," she said. "Even if we lost, it was still fun."

One of the cheerleaders was married. Gloria Tilman had met Dora resident Al Tilman when he was stationed with the military in California. After they married and he was sent overseas, Gloria moved from California to live with Al's family in Dora and finished high school there. "I had never even met his parents, but they took me in and became my family," she said. "They were marvelous."

Gloria and Al, who now live in Mountain View but winter in Texas, celebrated their 50th anniversary last April. "We girls didn't know a lot about cheerleading, but we just taught each other " said Gloria who has taught line dancing for several years. "We just did a lot of hopping and jumping around."

Team members acknowledged that it was sometimes disheartening after they'd lost yet another game during their first year. But team member Kelly Martin, now head of Martin Financial Services in Kansas City, noted that there was a silver lining to the otherwise trying experience. "The players and the cheerleaders rode on the same bus to the away games," he said. "And on the ride home, we got to sit with the girls. That back seat of the bus, it was the place to be."

© Copyright 2008 by www.ozarkcountytimes.com

DORA WINS 2020 STATE CHAMPIONSHIP
Falcons make Dora basketball history, win first ever Class 1 state championship

Dora Falcons: State champions!

Wednesday, March 18, 2020 • OZARK COUNTY TIMES • Page B1
By Kai Raymer www.OzarksSportsZone.com Reprinted with permission

The Dora Falcons earned the first state basketball championship in the school's history when they defeated St. Elizabeth 59-49 Friday, March 13, at JQH Arena in Springfield.

Photo by Karla Smith

Pictured, from left (front row): Seth Luna, Robbie Luna, Landon Luna, Auston Luna, Mason Luna, Damon Emery, Isaac Haney, Bryson Luna, Evan Smith, Trace Luna, Cayden Peck, Brylon Mayberry; (back row) assistant coach Curtis Warren, assistant coach Joshua Strong, Jacob Freiman, Tyler Luna, Bo Collins, Waylon Masters, Korey Murphy, Dylan Martin, Xavier Jewell, Spencer Howard and coach Rick Luna.

This time, they were tears of joy. Dora hoisted the first boys' basketball state champion- ship in program history Friday night with a 59-49 win over St. Elizabeth in the Class 1 finals at JQH Arena. Isaac Haney had a

OZARK COUNTY HEART
Boyhood Memories of a Dora Missouri Farm

game-high 25 points. Teammate Waylon Masters added 16 points, seven rebounds and vital post defense. The outcome was sweet redemption for a Falcons team that lost in the state title game a year ago. "Last year, I cried a lot," Masters said. "Honestly, I've cried more now. It's been so emotional. To experience what felt like the lowest point, then, to experience what feels like the highest point. It's wild. It was everything tonight." Dora's only other state title in school history came in 2009, when the Falcons won the Class 1 baseball crown. Rick Luna was the coach for that team and this one. But this time, he had his three sons – Bryson, Mason and Auston – on the floor in Dora's starting lineup. "It's good to win one for Dad," said Dora junior Bryson Luna. "He had to have us to get him here, but it's okay."

The Falcons' road to their first state championship was not easy. In the Class 1 playoffs, Dora beat four teams ranked in the top 10: South Iron (1), Jefferson (3), St. Elizabeth (4) and Delta (9)."That's hats off to these guys and the work they've put in all season long," said Dora coach Ri "We've always said: 'One goal, one. That's what we stick by. "Said Haney: "It encompasses the struggle we went through last year and all the hard work we put in to get back this year. Throughout the season, some of those big wins were steppingstones for us. The end-goal was ultimately to get back here." Jefferson beat Dora in the state finals a year ago, leaving the Falcons heartbroken. "I'm not a very good loser. And this bunch isn't either," Rick Luna said. "We try to be good losers. Anything we do, we try to come out on top, whether it's on the field or the court. The feeling is a lot better today." Against St. Elizabeth, Dora got some much-needed breathing room in the second half.

Haney hit a deep 3-pointer,and Bryson Luna followed ith a three-point play that put Dora up 46-34with five minutes remaining. St. Elizabeth, which was within four late in the third quarter, did not get the deficit under double digits again." (St. Elizabeth) did a good job of putting us in a half-court game," Rick Luna said. Dora went scoreless for a five-minute stretch from the first half into the second half. With its offense slowed, Dora dug in on defense. Masters helped the Falcons limit St. Elizabeth's 6'5" post duo, Brady Heckemeyer and Ross Struemph, to 11 points and 10 points, respectively. "We've really worked with (Masters) the last two weeks on his positioning – getting in front of post players – and then his help-side (defense) on the back," Rick Luna said. "He's a very high-IQ basketball player. What he's done the last few weeks... He overcomes a lot of size just by outsmarting a guy."

Dora 59, St. Elizabeth 49
Dora 14 12 10 23 — 59
St. Elizabeth 10 9 12 18 — 49

Dora (32-2 overall) – Isaac Haney 25, Waylon Masters 16, Bryson Luna 9, Mason Luna 8, Auston Luna 1.

IN MEMORIUM
James Windell Hall

Windell Hall, 93, died Sunday, February 12, 2017 at NHC Healthcare in West Plains. He was born Aug. 6, 1923, in Ozark County, the son of Frank Hall and Pearl Shipley Hall. He graduated from Bakersfield High School and earned a bachelor's degree from what is now Missouri State University in Springfield and a master's degree from the University of Missouri in Columbia. In 1947, he married May Canady. He began teaching in Ozark County early in life until duty to his country called. He served with the Army's 106th Infantry Division in the European theater during World War II. Upon his return, he continued his education and taught in the Dora and West Plains school systems until he retired at age 55 after 35 years of service. Teaching and working with students were among his greatest passions and enjoyment in life. He remained in touch with his students and peers throughout his years. Mr. Hall was a long-time member of the Ball Church of Christ in Dora; at the time of his death he was a member of Curry Street Church of Christ in West Plains. He is survived by May, his wife of 70 years; three children, Cynthia Morrison and husband Rayburn, Barry Hall and wife Rita, and Sue Lynn Collins and husband Richard; five grandchildren, Shaun Gentry, Nick Gentry, Kristi Huff, Misty Davis and Richelle Collins; two step-grandchildren, Mike Morrison and Rebecca Morrison Shelden; several great-grandchildren and step-great-grandchildren; one sister, Jewell Nicotra; and several nieces and nephews. He was preceded in death by his parents; five brothers, Sherman, Carl, Ralph, Hubey and Leo Hall; and one sister, Betty. Windell was buried in the Ball Cemetery. (Page 8 • OZARK COUNTY TIMES • Wednesday, February 15, 2017)

www.ingramcontent.com/pod-product-compliance
Lightning Source LLC
LaVergne TN
LVHW041543060526
838200LV00037B/1124